First World War
and Army of Occupation
War Diary
France, Belgium and Germany

59 DIVISION
176 Infantry Brigade
South Staffordshire Regiment
2/6th (T.F.) Battalion
24 February 1917 - 31 July 1918

WO95/3021/9

The Naval & Military Press Ltd
www.nmarchive.com
Published in association with The National Archives

Published by

The Naval & Military Press Ltd

Unit 10 Ridgewood Industrial Park,

Uckfield, East Sussex,

TN22 5QE England

Tel: +44 (0) 1825 749494

www.naval-military-press.com

www.nmarchive.com

This diary has been reprinted in facsimile from the original. Any imperfections are inevitably reproduced and the quality may fall short of modern type and cartographic standards.

© **Crown Copyright**
Images reproduced by permission of The National Archives, London, England, 2015.

Contents

Document type	Place/Title	Date From	Date To
Heading	WO95/3021/9		
Heading	59th Division 176th Infy Bde 2-6th Sth Staffs Regt. Feb 1917-Jly 1918 Also 1916 Jan Feb Disbanded Jly 18		
Heading	2/6th South Staffordshire Regiment February 1917 Vol 1		
War Diary	Bedford Wilts	24/02/1917	28/02/1917
Miscellaneous	R.4.d.5.4 R.4.d.5.4		
Heading	2/6th South Staffordshire Regiment March 1917 Vol II		
War Diary	Mericourt Sur Somme	01/03/1917	07/03/1917
War Diary	Foucaucourt	08/03/1917	29/03/1917
Heading	War Diary of 2/6th South Staffs Regiment From-30th March 1917 To-30th April 1917 Vol 3		
War Diary	Mons-in-Chausee	30/03/1917	02/04/1917
War Diary	Hancourt	03/04/1917	05/04/1917
War Diary	Montigny Fm	06/04/1917	17/04/1917
War Diary	Advance Parts	18/04/1917	30/04/1917
Heading	War Diary of 2/6th South Stafford Regiment From 1st May 1917 To 30th May 1917 Vol 4		
War Diary	Roisel	01/05/1917	03/05/1917
War Diary	Hamelet	04/05/1917	05/05/1917
War Diary	Ruelles Wd	06/05/1917	06/05/1917
War Diary	Gouance Posts	07/05/1917	14/05/1917
War Diary	Roisel	15/05/1917	19/05/1917
War Diary	Advanced Posts	19/05/1917	21/05/1917
War Diary	Roisel	23/05/1917	30/05/1917
Heading	War Diary of 2/6th South Stafford Regiment From 30th May 1917 To June 30th 1917 Vol 5		
War Diary	Roisel	30/05/1917	30/05/1917
War Diary	Equancourt	01/06/1917	10/06/1917
War Diary	Neuville	11/06/1917	22/06/1917
War Diary	Bourjonval	22/06/1917	30/06/1917
Heading	War Diary of 2/6th South Stafford Regiment From To July 1917 Vol 6		
War Diary		01/07/1917	02/07/1917
War Diary	Equancourt	02/07/1917	07/07/1917
War Diary	Barastre	08/07/1917	31/07/1917
Heading	War Diary of 2/6th Bn South Staffordshire Regiment From-1st August 1917 To-31st August 1917 Vol 7		
War Diary	Barastre	01/08/1917	23/08/1917
War Diary	Bouzincourt	30/08/1917	31/08/1917
Heading	War Diary of 2/6th Bn South Stafford Regiment From-1st Sept 1917 To-30th Sept 1917 Vol 8		
War Diary	Winnezeele	01/09/1917	01/09/1917
War Diary	Brandhoek	19/09/1917	20/09/1917
War Diary	Ypres North Area	20/09/1917	20/09/1917
War Diary	Front Line	20/09/1917	20/09/1917
War Diary	Goldfish Chateau (H 11 B 1,3)	20/09/1917	30/09/1917
Map	K.3.		
Miscellaneous	Message Form		

Heading	War Diary 2/6 South Staffordshire Regiment From 1st October 1917 To-31st October 1917 Vol 9		
War Diary	Ypres (East)	01/10/1917	01/10/1917
War Diary	Vlamertinghe	02/10/1917	02/10/1917
War Diary	Isbergues	07/10/1917	10/10/1917
War Diary	Aix Noulette	14/10/1917	21/10/1917
War Diary	Front Line	24/10/1917	30/10/1917
Heading	War Diary of 2/6th South Staffs Regiment From 1st Nov 1917 To 30th Nov 1917 Vol 10		
War Diary	Souchez	01/11/1917	19/11/1917
War Diary	Simencourt	20/11/1917	22/11/1917
War Diary	Courcelles-Le-Compte	23/11/1917	23/11/1917
War Diary	Heudecourt	24/11/1917	29/11/1917
War Diary	Bourlon Wood	29/11/1917	30/11/1917
Heading	War Diary of 2/6th South Staffs Regiment From 1st Dec 1917 To 31st Dec 1917 Vol 11		
War Diary	Bourlon Wood	01/12/1917	01/12/1917
War Diary	Flesquieres	02/12/1917	02/12/1917
War Diary	Ribecourt	03/12/1917	04/12/1917
War Diary	Havrincourt	05/12/1917	05/12/1917
War Diary	Ytres	06/12/1917	10/12/1917
War Diary	Rue	11/12/1917	31/12/1917
Heading	War Diary of 2/6th Bn South Staffs Regiment From 1st Jan 1918 To 31st Jan 1918 Vol 12		
War Diary	Rue	01/01/1918	22/01/1918
War Diary	Beaufort	23/01/1918	31/01/1918
Heading	War Diary of 2/6th Bn South Staffs Regiment From 1st Feb 1918 To 28th Feby 1918 Vol 13		
War Diary	Beaufort	01/02/1918	08/02/1918
War Diary	Pommier	09/02/1918	09/02/1918
War Diary	Mory	10/02/1918	28/02/1918
Heading	59th Division 176th Infantry Brigade War Diary 2/6th Battalion The South Staffordshire Regiment March 1918		
Heading	War Diary of 2/6th Bn South Staffs Regiment From 1st March 1918 To 31st March 1918 Vol 14		
War Diary		01/03/1918	31/03/1918
Heading	176th Brigade 59th Division 2/6th Battalion South Staffordshire Regiment April 1918		
Heading	War Diary of 2/6th Bn South Staffs Regiment From 1st April 1918 To 30th April 1918 Vol 15		
War Diary	Gauchin Legal	01/04/1918	01/04/1918
War Diary	Watou	02/04/1918	10/04/1918
War Diary	Ypres	11/04/1918	11/04/1918
War Diary	Passchendale	12/04/1918	13/04/1918
War Diary	Vlamertinghe	13/04/1918	13/04/1918
War Diary	Reninghelst	14/04/1918	14/04/1918
War Diary	Locre	15/04/1918	15/04/1918
War Diary	Bailluel	15/04/1918	15/04/1918
War Diary	Locre	16/04/1918	18/04/1918
War Diary	Terdeghem	19/04/1918	19/04/1918
War Diary	Elverdinghe	20/04/1918	21/04/1918
War Diary	Rousbrugge	22/04/1918	26/04/1918
War Diary	Poperinghe	26/04/1918	27/04/1918
War Diary	Reninghelst	28/04/1918	30/04/1918

Heading	War Diary 2/6th Battalion South Staffordshire Regiment (Training Cadre) From-May 1st 1918 To-May 31st 1918		
War Diary	Reninghelst	01/05/1918	05/05/1918
War Diary	Watou	06/05/1918	06/05/1918
War Diary	Lederzeele	07/05/1918	10/05/1918
War Diary	Mametz	11/05/1918	11/05/1918
War Diary	Fiefs	12/05/1918	14/05/1918
War Diary	Magnicourt-Le-Compte	15/05/1918	15/05/1918
War Diary	Somrin	16/05/1918	21/05/1918
War Diary	Magnicourt-Le-Compte	22/05/1918	22/05/1918
War Diary	Houdain	23/05/1918	29/05/1918
War Diary	Noyelles	30/05/1918	30/05/1918
War Diary	Buigny-St-Maclou	31/05/1918	31/05/1918
Heading	2/6th Battalion South Staffordshire Regiment (T.C) War Diary from June 1st 1918 to June 30th 1918 Vol		
War Diary	Buigny-St-Maclou	01/06/1918	07/06/1918
War Diary	Hellicourt	08/06/1918	17/06/1918
War Diary	Franleu	18/06/1918	19/06/1918
War Diary	Visse	20/06/1918	22/06/1918
War Diary	Bussus-Bussue	23/06/1918	30/06/1918
Heading	War Diary of 2/6th Battn South Staffordshire Regt. From 1st July 1918 To 31st July 1918 Vol 18		
War Diary	Bussus Bussuel	01/07/1918	20/07/1918
War Diary	Coquerel	21/07/1918	22/07/1918
War Diary	Lannoy-Guillere	23/07/1918	31/07/1918

W9q5/3021/a

59TH DIVISION
176TH INFY BDE

2-6TH STH STAFFS REGT
FEB 1917 ---- JLY 1918.

also 1916 Jan & Feb

DISBANDED JLY 18

2/6. Bun N. STAFF REG

1918

Army Form C. 2118.

Confidential

WAR DIARY
or
INTELLIGENCE SUMMARY

(Erase heading not required.)

126/9

Vol I

2/6th South Staffordshire Regiment

February 1917.

Place	Date	Hour	Summary of Events and Information	Remarks and references to Appendices

Instructions regarding War Diaries and Intelligence Summaries are contained in F. S. Regs., Part II. and the Staff Manual respectively. Title Pages will be prepared in manuscript.

2449 Wt. W14957/M90 750,000 1/16 J.B.C. & A. Forms/C.2118/12.

Army Form C. 2118.

WAR DIARY
or
INTELLIGENCE SUMMARY
(Erase heading not required.)

Instructions regarding War Diaries and Intelligence Summaries are contained in F.S. Regs., Part II. and the Staff Manual respectively. Title Pages will be prepared in manuscript.

Place	Date	Hour	Summary of Events and Information	Remarks and references to Appendices
Bedford Wilts	24-2-17		Instructions received under secret cover to embark at Southampton.	
do	25-2-17		Entrained at Bedford Station. Lt Col G.T. Affair in command, 31 Officers and 653 other ranks. Arrived Southampton 11-30 a.m. Embarked on H.M.T. VIPER at 4 P.M.	
	26-2-17		Disembarked at HAVRE at 9 a.m. and proceeded to No. 5. Rest Camp. Entrained at midnight and proceeded to SALEUX arriving there at 4 P.M. and Billeted there for the night.	
	27-2-17		Proceeded by march to FOUILLOY and Billeted there for the night.	
	28-2-17		Transport party & first line transport rejoined Unit on this march from GLISY.	

Asked
Lt Colonel
Commanding
2/6 South Staffordshire Regt.

"B" Coy.   R.4.d.54.
"C" Coy.   R.4.d.54.
"D" Coy.   MUDDY LANE POST
Battn. HQ.   L.35.d.80.

Guides will meet Platoons en route
Company Commanders are again warned
of the necessity of reporting completion of
relief of their Companies to B.H.Q. This
should be done with the minimum amount of
delay. Code word "NIL RETURN".

All Trench Stores defence schemes maps
and aeroplane photos will be handed
over and receipts taken. Receipts will
be handed in Bn. H.Q. by 10.0 a.m.
tomorrow 30th September.

R.A.Blunden
Capt A/Adjt
26th Bn. R.W. Fus.

Army Form C. 2118.

Confidential Original

WAR DIARY
or
INTELLIGENCE SUMMARY

(Erase heading not required.)

2/6th South Staffordshire Regiment.

March 1917.

Vol II

P. 2

Army Form C. 2118.

Confidential

WAR DIARY
—or—
INTELLIGENCE SUMMARY
(Erase heading not required.)

Instructions regarding War Diaries and Intelligence Summaries are contained in F.S. Regs., Part II. and the Staff Manual respectively. Title Pages will be prepared in manuscript.

Place	Date	Hour	Summary of Events and Information	Remarks and references to Appendices
MERICOURT SUR SOMME	MARCH 1st		The Battalion proceeded by Route March to MERICOURT-SUR-SOMME and were billeted in Huts.	
	2nd to 7th		The Battalion remained at MERICOURT-SUR-SOMME. The training of all Specialists was continued. The Advance Party who had been attached to the 9th DURHAM LIGHT INFANTRY for instruction rejoined the Battalion on the 2nd March.	
FOUCAUCOURT.	8th		The Battalion proceeded by Route March to FOUCAUCOURT and were again billeted in Huts. On this day the Battalion became Battalion in Brigade Reserve.	
	9th		Two Officers and one Platoon from each Company proceeded to front line and were attached to the 2/5th North Staffordshire Regiment for Instruction. Several enemy H.E. shells fell near the mens Huts and exploded without causing casualties.	
	10th		The Battalion relieved the 2/5th North Staffordshire Regt in front line Sector immediately South of GENERMONT (Map reference Sheet 62 C.S.W. Section 3A) from T.15.a.3.7. to T.9.B.8.7. These trenches were held by the Battalion until the night of the 14th March. No operations were undertaken either by the Battalion or the enemy on this front during this period. Enemy snipers were busy the whole time. B Company had 4 casualties on the 13th March. Rain fell heavily on two nights. Communication and front line trenches were very wet and muddy in some places the mud being knee deep. Great difficulty was experienced in getting the rations and rations owing to the mud and the men were very exhausted.	
	14th		The Battalion were relieved by the 2/5th North Staffordshire Regt and went into support trenches at BERNY	
	15th		Owing to the exhausted condition of the men and the number of sick the Battalion	

2449 Wt. W14957/Mgo 750,000 1/16 J.B.C. & A. Forms/C.2118/12.

Confidential

Army Form C. 2118.

WAR DIARY
or
INTELLIGENCE SUMMARY

(Erase heading not required.)

Instructions regarding War Diaries and Intelligence Summaries are contained in F. S. Regs., Part II. and the Staff Manual respectively. Title Pages will be prepared in manuscript.

Place	Date	Hour	Summary of Events and Information	Remarks and references to Appendices
	MARCH 15th		were relieved by the 2/6th the Sherwood Foresters and proceeded by march to FOUCAUCOURT where they were billeted in huts being temporarily attached to the 178th Infantry Brigade	
	16th		Lieutenant Colonel G.J. Spier handed over command of the Battalion to Major G. Stuart Wortley, the men were engaged cleaning clothing and equipment and making up deficiencies.	
	17th and 18th 19th		The Battalion were engaged cleaning clothing and equipment and making up deficiencies. Orders received for the Battalion to move on the 20th March and occupy the old front line trenches at Genermont	
	20th		The Battalion marched to GENERMONT and occupied the Dugouts in the old front line trenches south of GENERMONT.	
	21st 22nd and 23rd		All available strength engaged on Divisional Lines of Communication remarking the BERNY – FRESNES – MISERY Road	
	23rd		The Battalion moved forward and occupied the German Dugouts at FRESNES.	
	24th 25th and 26th		All available strength engaged as on 21st 22nd & 23rd	
	27th		The Battalion moved forward and occupied the German Dugouts between MAZENCOURT and MISERY	
	28th		The Battalion marched from MISERY to MONS-EN-CHAUSSEE and were billetted there in Cellars. All Houses, wells and fruit Trees in this town were destroyed by the enemy before their retirement.	

Army Form C. 2118.

WAR DIARY
or
INTELLIGENCE SUMMARY

(Erase heading not required.)

Instructions regarding War Diaries and Intelligence Summaries are contained in F. S. Regs., Part II. and the Staff Manual respectively. Title Pages will be prepared in manuscript.

Confidential

Place	Date	Hour	Summary of Events and Information	Remarks and references to Appendices
	MARCH 29th		One Officer and 60 other ranks engaged on Divisional Lines of Communication, repairing the BRIE – PRUSLE Road at P.25.c.2.4, where enemy mine had been sprung. The remainder of the Battalion were engaged clearing out cellars at MONS-en-CHAUSSEE.	
	30-3-17.			

(signature)
Lieut-Colonel
Commanding
1/6 South Staffordshire Regt.

Army Form C. 2118.

WAR DIARY
or
INTELLIGENCE SUMMARY.
(Erase heading not required.)

Summary of Events and Information | Remarks and references to Appendices

Confidential

Original War Diary
of
2/6th South Staffs Regiment

From – 30th March 1917
To – 30th April 1917

Army Form C. 2118.

Confidential

WAR DIARY
or
INTELLIGENCE SUMMARY
(Erase heading not required.)

Instructions regarding War Diaries and Intelligence Summaries are contained in F.S. Regs., Part II. and the Staff Manual respectively. Title Pages will be prepared in manuscript.

Place	Date	Hour	Summary of Events and Information	Remarks and references to Appendices
Hameau Channels	20/3/17	—	One party consisting of 1 Officer 150 other ranks at work under R.E. instructors.	
do		—	do 20 other ranks do	
do	31/3/17	—	do 3 Officers & 150 other ranks do	
do		—	One party consisting of 3 Officers & 150 other ranks at work under R.E. instructors do 20 other ranks	
do	1/4/17	—	Church parade in morning. One party consisting of one Officer & 55 other ranks at work under R.E. instructors	
do	2/4/17	—	Battalion marched to Hancourt 16.20 a.m. One party consisting of 1 Officer & 10 Officer Infantry 8.30 a.m. arrived at Hancourt. Work under R.E. instructors of 50 other ranks at work under R.E.	
Hancourt	3/4/17	—	One party consisting of 10 Officers & 155 other ranks on R.E. work. Remainder available	
do	4/4/17	—	One party consisting of 4 Officers & 220 other ranks on work under R.E. & further consisting in all of 4 Officers on reserve line at work on trench mats. We put in grand Remainder at Batt at work at training etc about 4 prs 3/1/17. over on at our own aerodrome which adjoined R.E. at training.	
do	5/4/17	10.30 a.m.	Batt arrived at new position at H 35 d 9.9. Shelled by H.E. and Shrapnel during the afternoon.	
Moislains	6/4/17		Two Companies engaged digging advanced pts. P at H 26 a 75 killed by H.E. +20 men	
	7/4/17		wounded. Any efforts 4.0 mm at work under R.E. Supervision.	
	8/4/17	11.45	Patrol reported enemy retirement on haste along true Bolson	
	9/4/17		of 65 Regular + 1 stab tisha Numbers in enemy trueline 5 road of village. E "63" ahead S. and	
	10/4/17		of harasoil reed and rifle + M.G. fire & Lay Numbers in	
			Batt: prompt support, troops & 4 Tuesday	
	11/4/17		Batt: 185th Stop Col 7 Light Flench Prey of opp one comp in reserve	
	12/4/17		183 ad Br 8 Stop Col 29 Light Preyle H. A. killed. rested	
	13/4/17		14/4/17 One of our aeroplane fallen hospital down by hostile + Lowered	
	14/4/17		2 aeroplane at work under R.E. Supervision.	
	15/4/17		Batt move up to trenches in support J H.6 at L.21 d 95.6 + 27 d 80.	
	16/4/17		Relieved 11.6. in advance posts	
	17/4/17		"P.84" our M.G. in flames in flames during the	
			evenings. 5.8 again passed pr pr of tuesand	
			evening Observed another enemy aeroplane in flames shot	
			down by hostile aeroplane in flames shot	

WAR DIARY or INTELLIGENCE SUMMARY

Army Form C. 2118.

(Erase heading not required.)

Place	Date	Hour	Summary of Events and Information	Remarks and references to Appendices
Advanced Posts	19/9/17 20/9/17		Patrols sent out found touch with enemy. Enemy artillery very active.	
	21/9/17		Our patrols sent out these & after having come in contact with enemy patrols which were captured. Advance posts at L.23.c.7.4 & L.28.c.5.7. noted. Two pts at L.30.A.12 & Souchy post L.30.A.13 dug.	
	22/9/17		Enemy after posts advanced by patrol at L.24.c.1.9. Our Bn. relieved by R.E. & took up position in support. Posts from L.20.c.0.3 to L.21.A.9.5. Some aerial activity on front of the enemy. Enemy guns throughout in support.	
	23/9/17		Enemy artillery quiet. Enemy O.P. observed at L.24.c.2.5. Enemy O.S. balloon Westgarten by us at 5.30 p.m.	
	24/9/17		3 Off, 95 O.R. employed digging new running from L.20.c.0.0. to L.22.c.0.3. 4 L.20.a.0.0 to L.20.a.0.4. Enemy 10. 3 your enemy destroyed by enemy R.E. Junior Tr. R.E. 16. 7 Shooting 10. 3 your enemy destroyed by enemy H.E. Junior turned signal turning with pts. Being artillery active. Survived rest at L.20 & 43 throughout. Balloon above R.E. in advance posts.	
	25/9/17		Post improvements strengthened. Enemy scout enplanal at 6 a.m. Enemy artillery quiet. Enemy scout at L.20.4.4.5. shelled infantry by himself. Advance posts were improved.	
	26/9/17		Pat M.G. at L.24.c.4.3 heavily shelled, also trenches at L.23.c.2.9. Enemy also advance posts - advance from heavily shelled. Being on Belliv shaved in advance posts by L.J. & moved to point 62.	
	27/9/17		Men employed cleaning up & fetching up V.L. Stores started in L.G. Sniping recovery.	
	28/9/17			
	29/9/17			
	30/9/17			

Army Form C. 2118.

WAR DIARY
~~INTELLIGENCE SUMMARY~~
(Erase heading not required.)

Instructions regarding War Diaries and Intelligence Summaries are contained in F. S. Regs., Part II. and the Staff Manual respectively. Title Pages will be prepared in manuscript.

Place	Date	Hour	Summary of Events and Information	Remarks and references to Appendices
				Vol 4
				Miss West
				P.4

Original.

Confidential

2/6TH

War Diary

of

South Stafford Regiment

From :- 1st May 1917
To :- 30th May, 1917

Army Form C. 2118.

WAR DIARY
or
INTELLIGENCE SUMMARY
(Erase heading not required.)

May 1917

Instructions regarding War Diaries and Intelligence Summaries are contained in F.S. Regs., Part II and the Staff Manual respectively. Title Pages will be prepared in manuscript.

Place	Date	Hour	Summary of Events and Information	Remarks and references to Appendices
ROISEL	1/5/17		Two Officers and 100 men working under Town Major ROISEL	
do	2/5/17	9 p.m.	ROISEL shelled by enemy with H.E. Six Officers 330 O.R. working under R.E. supervision	
do	3/5/17	9-10	Men employed cleaning up town & digging public latrines	
HAMELET	4.5.17		Battalion + Baker H.Q. moved to HAMELET	
	6.5.17		2 Officers 150 O.R. working under R.E. supervision. Enemy aircraft very active	
			Enemy having been reported to be concentrating at "YALAKOIS" F" Battalion moved into support at ROISEL	
RUELLES WR	6.5.17		Two companies "E" + "W" moved two companies 2/4 Sherwood Foresters in support at Ruelles Wood. All available men engaged wiring or means line of resistance.	
ADVANCE POSTS	7.5.17		Two companies A + B relieved two companies 2/6 North Staffords on Advance Posts. Men engaged improving Advance Posts held. This was continued on 8th & 9th instant.	
do	10.5.17		Battalion relieved 2/6 North Staffords in front line	
do	11.5.17		Our artillery very active, heavily bombarding enemy front line. Our fathers active. All available men employed carrying R.E. stores up to front line and improving and extending of trenches. Wiring in front of Advance Posts. Our Left in Lunacy (L.8.U.9.2) heavily shelled with 5" 9's.	
		3-10 p.m.	One of our aeroplanes driven down by enemy. Pilot unwounded in 1st am got safely into our front line.	
	12.5.17		One fired at L.11.b9.9 heavily shelled with whiz-bangs + H.E. Wiring in front of HINDENBURG LINE.	
	13.5.17	6.35 a.m.	HARCOURT heavily shelled with H.E. Enemy snipers active. Many cases of enemy working in front of advanced posts and improvement of trenches continued.	
	14.5.17		Our Battalion relieved by 2/5 North Staffords in front line. Enemy watching again. One big working on Main line of Resistance.	

2449 Wt. W14957/M90 750,000 1/16 J.B.C. & A. Forms/C.2118/12.

Army Form C. 2118.

WAR DIARY
or
INTELLIGENCE SUMMARY

(Erase heading not required.)

Hargicourt   May 1917

Place	Date	Hour	Summary of Events and Information	Remarks and references to Appendices
ADVANCE POSTS (A.85)	15.5.17		Working in front of Advance Post position and improvement of trenches continued, 4 showers trenches tuned.	
ROISEL	18.5.17 19.5.17		Specialist training continued. Men employed digging and wiring on 3rd Zone of Resistance under R.E. supervision.	
ADVANCED POSTS	19.5.17 20.5.17 20.5.17		Un battalion moved from ROISEL and relieved 2/6 North Staffords in Front Line Outposts &c. Emichrants and cutting on both sides. All available men wiring in front of Advanced Posts under R.E. supervision. Trenches improved and extended.	
	21.5.17 5.40 p.m.		Enemy artillery active. HARGICOURT heavily shelled also artillery O.Ps. All available men employed every evening improving wiring &c.	
ROISEL	23/24 5.17.		Un battalion relieved in Advanced Posts by Lincolnshire Dragoons and central trucks. Horse and moved to ROISEL.	
	24.5.30 5.17		Men employed bathing + cleaning up. Working parties as strong as possible proceeding nightly to work on wiring in front of Main Line of Resistance under R.E supervision. Specialist training continued.	

Winchester for
2/6. Lord Stafford.

Army Form C. 2118.

WAR DIARY
or
INTELLIGENCE SUMMARY

(Erase heading not required.)

Instructions regarding War Diaries and Intelligence Summaries are contained in F. S. Regs., Part II. and the Staff Manual respectively. Title Pages will be prepared in manuscript.

Place	Date	Hour	Summary of Events and Information	Remarks and references to Appendices

Vol 5

Original

Confidential

War Diary
of
2/6th South Stafford Regiment

From 30th May 1917

to - June 30th 1917

P.5

Army Form C. 2118.

WAR DIARY
or
INTELLIGENCE SUMMARY

(Erase heading not required.)

CONFIDENTIAL JUNE 1917.

Instructions regarding War Diaries and Intelligence Summaries are contained in F.S. Regs., Part II and the Staff Manual respectively. Title Pages will be prepared in manuscript.

Map reference 62c NE.
Sheets 57/12 SE. 57c NE.

Place	Date	Hour	Summary of Events and Information	Remarks and references to Appendices
ROISEL	May 30		Battalion moved to EQUANCOURT — The Units MARQUAIX — AIZECOURT LE BAS — NURLU — EQUANCOURT. Battalion into Divisional Reserve under canvas at VILLA O.A.	
EQUANCOURT	June 1 –4		Infantry training carried on and specialists trained.	
	5.		Brigade sports held at VILLA O.A.	
			B & C Companies moved to NEUVILLE BOURJONVAL and worked under Corps troops for four days.	
	June 9.		A & D Companies relieved B & C Companies at NEUVILLE BOURJONVAL and carried out the same duties.	
	" 10.		Battalion relieved the 2/4 Sherwood Foresters in Outpost at NEUVILLE.	
NEUVILLE BOURJONVAL	" 11 June 22		Available men in working parties digging C.T.s for HAVRINCOURT WOOD to front line.	
	June 22		A & B Companies relieved by 2/4 York & Lancs Battalion & kept in support as Battalion.	
			Battalion relieved 2/6 North Staffs Regt. in the Brigade left sub. sector in Q5 c and d.	
	June 23		Front line trench and HAVRINCOURT WOOD shelled with 4.2".	
	June 24		Men employed in improving trenches — digging dutches and latrines.	
	" 25		Enemy artillery active & much battery shelled, some BILHEM FARM shelled with 4.2".	
		10.30p.m.	4th Bn. front line and support trenches shelled by trench mortars and 77 m.m. air Nobles.	
	" 26.		Battery again enfiladed in trench vary south. Our support line and BILHEM FARM shelled with 4.2" to 10.30 p.m. — Enemy machine gun active training on parapets.	
	" 27.		FINS and HAVRINCOURT WOOD heavily shelled. Low communication trench front line shelled by 4.9 minnies. German O.P. noticed & our gunners at K3b d.0.2. — artillery replied to it and obtained two direct hits.	
	" 28.		12 to 12.30 A.m. front line in Q5d shelled with 4.2". Enemy were heard at L26c and d.	

Army Form C. 2118.

WAR DIARY
or
INTELLIGENCE SUMMARY
(Erase heading not required.)

Instructions regarding War Diaries and Intelligence Summaries are contained in F. S. Regs., Part II. and the Staff Manual respectively. Title Pages will be prepared in manuscript.

Place	Date	Hour	Summary of Events and Information	Remarks and references to Appendices
~~NEUVE~~	June 29		Front line trench shelled by MINNENWERFERS. 7-7.54 – shelled 17th displaying 2. 3.1 –. Enemy battery spotted by our observer. Enemy O.P. observed at L.35.6.37.	
	June 30		Enemy artillery quiet. Each night for the 23 June to 1st July aggressive patrols left our lines no enemy patrols were encountered.	

A Hurst Winter
Lt. Col.
Commanding 2/6 North Staffs
Staffordshire Regiment

Army Form C. 2118.

WAR DIARY
or
INTELLIGENCE SUMMARY

(Erase heading not required.)

Instructions regarding War Diaries and Intelligence Summaries are contained in F. S. Regs., Part II. and the Staff Manual respectively. Title Pages will be prepared in manuscript.

Place	Date	Hour	Summary of Events and Information	Remarks and references to Appendices
				Vol 6
				Confidential
				P.6
			Original	
			War Diary	
			of	
			2/6TH South Stafford Regiment	
			From:—	
			To:— July 1917	

2449 Wt. W4957/M90 750,000 1/16 J.B.C. & A. Forms/C.2118/12.

Army Form C. 2118.

Confidential

WAR DIARY
or
INTELLIGENCE SUMMARY

(Erase heading not required.)

2/6 South Staffordshire Regiment

July 1917.

Instructions regarding War Diaries and Intelligence Summaries are contained in F. S. Regs., Part II. and the Staff Manual respectively. Title Pages will be prepared in manuscript.

Place	Date	Hour	Summary of Events and Information	Remarks and references to Appendices
	1917 July 1st		Enemy artillery active HAVRINCOURT WOOD heavily shelled.	
	1, 2nd		Relieved in front line trenches by 2/6 Warwickshire Regiment and then went	
			proceeded to EQUANCOURT and had motor busses at that place	
EQUANCOURT	July 1st, 7th		Battalion employed in cleaning up. Special training commenced and having	
	7th July		3 specialists carried on with.	
			Battalion moved into bivouac at O 11 E near BARASTRE Sheet 57c S.W.	
			travelling via LECHELLE-BUS-BARASTRE	
BARASTRE	8th July		Battalion employed on infantry camp.	
	9th "		Various training carried on. Specialist training continued. Lectures on	
	10th "		touch and go control.	
	11th-14th "		Battalion sports held. Also dress rehearsals for the Battalion at Divisional	
			Sports to be held on the 22nd July	
	15th July		Various training and tactical exercises carried out.	
	21st "			
	22nd July		Divisional Sports held.	
	23rd "		Continued training including Musketry & Specialist training	
	24-26 "			
	27th "		Divisional tactical scheme carried out over SOMME battle field	
	28 "		near SAILLY-SAILLISEL	

Confidential   July 1917

Army Form C. 2118.

WAR DIARY
or
INTELLIGENCE SUMMARY 2/6 South Staffordshire Regiment

(Erase heading not required.)

Place	Date	Hour	Summary of Events and Information	Remarks and references to Appendices
BARASTRE	29th 30th		Church Parade held on 29th. Training carried on as usual.	
	31 July		Brigade tactical exercise carried out near HAPLINCOURT. During the month opportunity was given to Officers went once to AMIENS, and leave to ENGLAND was reallotted.	Strength of 1: Off. Coming 2/Lt. I. Stafford Reg

Army Form C. 2118.

WAR DIARY
or
INTELLIGENCE SUMMARY
(Erase heading not required.)

Vol 7

Confidential

P.7

Original

War Diary
of
2/6th Bn South Staffordshire Regiment

From 1st August 1917
to 31st August 1917

Army Form C. 2118.

WAR DIARY
or
INTELLIGENCE SUMMARY

(Erase heading not required.)

Instructions regarding War Diaries and Intelligence Summaries are contained in F. S. Regs., Part II. and the Staff Manual respectively. Title Pages will be prepared in manuscript.

Sheet 1.

Place	Date	Hour	Summary of Events and Information	Remarks and references to Appendices
BARASTRE.	1. Aug.		The Battalion was in Camp under canvas.	
	13th Aug.		Training took place daily. 176th Infantry Brigade Sports were held.	
	23rd Aug.		The Battalion moved to BOUZINCOURT (Map reference Sheet 57.D.) by motor bus and route march via OVILLERS, LA BOISELLE, and AVELUY. The first half of the journey was made by motor bus and the second half the Battalion route marched, arriving at BOUZINCOURT at 4.30.p.m. 23rd. August. The Battalion was billeted at cottages and farm houses. Training was continued.	
BOUZINCOURT	30th Aug.		The Battalion was ordered to move to WINNEZEELE (Sheet HAZEBROUCK) on the 30th August but the move was postponed for 24 hours.	
	31st Aug.		The Battalion less one Company left BOUZINCOURT at 8.10.a.m. 31st Aug. and entrained at AVELUY at 9.a.m. arriving at HOPOUTRE near POPERINGHE (Sheet HAZEBROUCK) at 10.p.m. 31st Aug. After detraining the Battalion left HOPOUTRE at 12 midnight and marched to Camp at WINNEZEELE via ABEELE and STEENVORDE, arriving in camp at 5. a.m. 1st September. One Company entrained at AVELUY at 8.p.m 31st August and arrived at WINNEZEELE at 7.p.m. 1st Sept.	
	2...9...17.			

[signature]
LIEUT. COLONEL.
Commanding 2/6th Battalion South Staffordshire Regiment.

Army Form C. 2118.

WAR DIARY
or
INTELLIGENCE SUMMARY.

(Erase heading not required.)

Vol 8

Confidential

Original
War Diary
of
2/6th Bn South Stafford Regiment

From :- 1st Sept 1917
To :- 30th Sept 1917

Army Form C. 2118.

WAR DIARY
or
INTELLIGENCE SUMMARY

(Erase heading not required.)

Instructions regarding War Diaries and Intelligence Summaries are contained in F.S. Regs., Part II. and the Staff Manual respectively. Title Pages will be prepared in manuscript.

SHEET 1

Place	Date	Hour	Summary of Events and Information	Remarks and references to Appendices
			References - Maps HAZEBROUCK 5a, BELGIUM Sheet 28, BELGIUM Sheet 28 N3E3 SHEET K3.	
WINNEZEELE	1 Sept	5 a.m.	The Battalion arrived in Camp at WINNEZEELE at 5 a.m. 1st September 1917, Training was continued.	
BRANDHOEK	19 Sept		The Battalion moved by march and bus from WINNEZEELE TO BRANDHOEK No1 Area (G 6 d central Sheet 28) The Camp at WINNEZEELE was left at 10.30 a.m. and the Battalion proceeded via STEENVORDE and main YPRES Road arriving in new area at 4.30 p.m. 19h September.	
BRANDHOEK	20 Sept		At 4.30 on the afternoon of the 20th September the Battalion moved ready for Battle to the YPRES North Area. (H 11 b 1,3) where it came under the orders of the G.O.C. 55th Division. The Battalion moves under the Command of Lieut, Colonel J Stuart Wortley and Major H.M.C. Curtis was in Command of all details who remained at BRANDHOEK No 1 Area.	
YPRES North Area.			On the night 20/21 Sept the Battalion moved to and took up a position in the Old British Front Line to the EAST of OXFORD ROAD (C 29 c) and Headquarters were established at WARWICK FARM. During the afternoon of the 21st Sept Major H.M.C. Curtis took over the Command of the Battalion. From the Old British Front Line the battalion relieved the 165th Infantry Brigade on the night 22/23 Sept in the right sector of the line held by the 55th Division, and were supported by the 2/5h Bn, South Staffordshire Regiment The disposition of the Battalion was as follows:- Headquarters POMMERN CASTLE (C 19 a 5 4.) "B" Company on the right (Southern Area) "A" Company in the centre at HILL 37 . "B" Company on the left in the CAPITOL Area and "C" Company in support at ELMS COURT. Consolidation of the front line was rapidly proceeded with as an advance had been made by the 165th Infantry Brigade on the morning of the 21st.	(See map K23)
FRONT LINE			On the night 23/24 September a heavy hostile artillery barrage preceeded an attempted hostile counter attack. Sentries of this Unit reported that the enemy were preparing to attack. After waiting for developments and making preparations to repel the attack the S.O.S. signal was given and artillery support was at once forthcoming The Company in support at ELMS CORNER then moved forward to reinforce the Front line, but the attack did not develope. Slight casualties were sustained, On the night of the 24/25 September this Unit was relieved in the front line by the 2/4 Leicesters 2/5 Leicesters and the 2/6 Sherwoods. The Unit then returned to Camp at GOLDFISH CHATEAU YPRES North Area arriving there at 2 a.m. on the morning of the 25th September.	
GOLDFISH CHATEAU (H 11 b 1,3)			At 11 p.m. 25th September the Battalion moved to the Old British Front Line EAST of OXFORD ROAD under the Command of Lieut, Colonel J Stuart Wortley, Battalion Headquarters were at WARWICK FARM and the Battalion was in position by 4 a.m. 26th Sept ready to give immediate support to the attacking units of the 59th Division.	

Army Form C. 2118.

WAR DIARY
or
INTELLIGENCE SUMMARY
(Erase heading not required.)

SHEET 11.

Instructions regarding War Diaries and Intelligence Summaries are contained in F.S. Regs., Part II. and the Staff Manual respectively. Title Pages will be prepared in manuscript.

Place	Date	Hour	Summary of Events and Information	Remarks and references to Appendices
	28/29 Sept		At 5 p.m. 26th Sept orders were received for the Battalion to move forward, Headquarters were established at POMMERN CASTLE and the four Companies entrenched WEST of POMMERN CASTLE Immediate support to the Battalion in the line was not required and this unit was ordered to take up the position previously held in Old British Front Line and arrived there at 1.30 a.m. on the morning of the 28th September. On the night 28/29 Sept this Unit relieved the 2/8 and 2/7 Sherwoods in the left sector of the Divisional front. The dispositions of Companies was :- "A"Company C 14 b 9,9, to C 14 b 2,3(Sheet 28) to a depth of 250 yards to TORONTO inclusive and in touch with the 2/6th North Staffordshire Regiment on the left flank. "D" Company took over the central forward area C 14 a 6,9, to C 14 a 7,3, in depth 250 yards "B" and "C" mpanies took over the rear forward area from c 13 b 9,9, to C 14 a 2,2 (Kansas Cross) to a depth of about 300 yards. Battalion Headquarters were at CORNHILL C 18 d 2,9.	
	29/30Sept.		This Unit was relieved in the front line by No 2 Company and half of No 13 Company of the 2nd Canterbury Battalion and on relief occupied a position in the Old British Front line EAST of OXFORD ROAD During the time the Battalion was in the front line and in immediate support the Casualties averaged about 20%.	
	6/10/17.			

signature LIEUT. COLONEL,
COMMANDING 2/6TH BN, SOUTH STAFFORDSHIRE REGIMENT.

1:10 000   K.3.   EDITION I.   Parts of { 28 N.E. / 28 N.W.

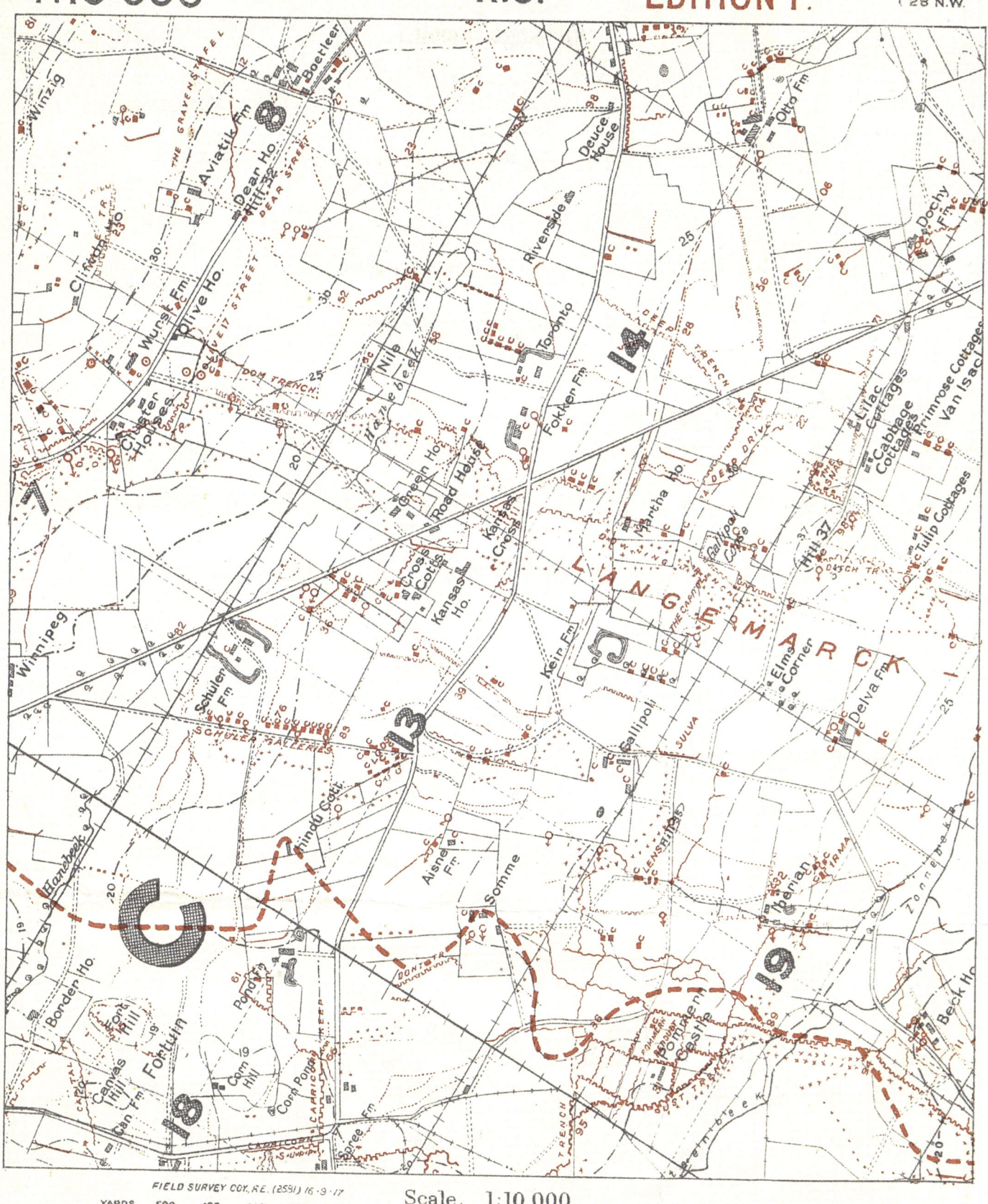

FIELD SURVEY COY. R.E. (2591) 16·9·17   Scale. 1:10,000.

Message Form.

...................Division.

Map reference or mark own position on Map at back.

1. I am at..

2. I am at..and am consolidating.

3. I am at..and have consolidated.

4. I need :—Ammunition.
   Bombs.
   Rifle Grenades.
   Water.
   Very lights.
   Stokes shells.

5. Enemy forming up for counter-attack at....... ....

6. I am in touch with............................... on Right/Left at ....

7. I am not in touch on Right/Left

8. Am being shelled from...

9. I estimate my present strength at ....rifles.

10. Hostile {Battery / Machine Gun / Trench Mortar} active at..

Time..........................a.m. (p.m.)   Name..

Date...................................   Platoon................. Company...........

Place..................................   Battalion...................................

Army Form C. 2118.

WAR DIARY
or
INTELLIGENCE SUMMARY
(Erase heading not required.)

Vol 9

P.9

CONFIDENTIAL

WAR DIARY.

2/6 SOUTH STAFFORDSHIRE REGIMENT

FROM 1st OCTOBER 1917 TO 31st OCTOBER 1917.

Place	Date	Hour	Summary of Events and Information	Remarks and references to Appendices

Army Form C. 2118.

Instructions regarding War Diaries and Intelligence Summaries are contained in F.S. Regs., Part II. and the Staff Manual respectively. Title Pages will be prepared in manuscript.

WAR DIARY
or
INTELLIGENCE SUMMARY

(Erase heading not required.)

SHEET 1.

Reference Maps:- BELGIUM Sheet 28 : HAZEBROUCK 5a : LENS 11 : LENS 36.c.S.W.1. ; FRANCE Sheet 36c. :

OCTOBER 1917.

Place	Date	Hour	Summary of Events and Information	Remarks and references to Appendices
YPRES (EAST)	1st Oct.		On the 1st October 1917 this Unit moved from the OLD BRITISH FRONT LINE (BELGIUM Sheet 28. C.29.c.) to Camp SOUTH of Railway at VLAMERTINGHE at 6.30.p.m.	
VLAMERTINGHE	2nd Oct		The Battalion less Transport entrained at VLAMERTINGHE at 10.a.m. and Detrained at THIENNES (HAZEBROUCK 5a) at 4.15.p.m. The Battalion marched to ISBERGUES near AIRE (HAZEBROUCK 5a) and was billeted in the district. Headquarters were established at MOULBRUN and Company training was continued.	
ISBERGUES	7th Oct.		On the 7th Oct. the Battalion moved from the ISBERGUES district to FONTAINES LES BOULANS (LENS 11) The first part of the journey was by motor bus and the second part by route march the Unit arriving in billets at 2.30.p.m. Training was in progress when orders were received for the Battalion to move nearer the line.	
	10th Oct.		From FONTAINES LES BOULANS the Unit moved by motor bus to BOIS du PROISSART.(Sheet 36c.3.) near BRUAY and Barlin. Headquarters were at C.18.a.7.3. (Sheet 363)	
AIX – NOULETTE	14th Oct.		On the afternoon of the 14th Oct. the Battalion left Camp at BOIS du PROISSART and marched to NOULETTE HUTS (Sheet 363. R.27.b.2.5.) entering the Huts at dusk. The Quartermaster's Stores and Transport were billeted in the village of BOUVIGNY BOYEFFLES. The Battalion remained in Camp at NOULETTE Huts until 21st October during which time the roads and paths approaching the Camp were repaired and improved, the huts especially the roofs were repaired and the Camp improved generally.	
	16th Oct.		During the morning of the 16th Oct. one Company moved forward to prepare billets in LIEVIN (LENS 36c.S.W.1.) Working parties were found on the nights of 18th, and 19th Oct. Both nights the parties worked under R.E. supervision on the Communication Trenches known as CROCODILE Trench and ABSOLUM Trench (Sheet 36c.S.W.1. – M.24.c & b.)	
	21st Oct.		On the night of 21/22 Oct the Unit relieved the 2/5th Bn, South Staffordshire Regiment in the right sub-section of the 176th Infantry Brigade Front. The front line was held by two Companies and extended from N.20.c.0.5. to N.20.c.0.1. (Sheet 36c.S.W.1.) Three Companies proceeded by train on the Light Railway as far as WHIZBANG CORNER (M.22.d.4.6.) The Company which was previously stationed in LIEVIN proceeded by route march to take up a position in support at M.30.a.8.3. Battalion Headquarters were at M.30.a.4.9. and the Reserve Company at M.30.a.8.3. in cellars.	

Army Form C. 2118.

WAR DIARY
or
INTELLIGENCE SUMMARY

(Erase heading not required.)

Place	Date	Hour	Summary of Events and Information	Remarks and references to Appendices
FRONT LINE	24th Oct,		On the night of 24/25th Oct, the two Companies in the Front Line were relieved by the companies in Support and Reserve respectively.	
	25th Oct,		At 11,P,m, on the night of 25th/26th Oct "O" Special Company R,E, carried out a successful GAS ATTACK in the sector immediately on the right of this Unit's front, Gas was discharged for about a quarter of an hour and the attack was supported by Divisional Artillery and a Heavy Artillery Group, During the eight days in the line the Battalion sustained only nine casualties, 2/Lt H,R,HAMILTON was severely wounded,	
	29th Oct,		On the night 29/30th October the Unit was relieved by the 2/5th Bn, LINCOLN REGIMENT of the 177th Infantry Brigade, The relief was speedy and was completed without incident, On being relieved the Battalion proceeded by platoons to Camp at SOUCHEZ (Sheet 36c,S,W, - S,8,a,3,1,)	
	30th Oct,		The day was spent in cleaning arms and equipment, On the night 30/31 Oct and during the day of 31st Oct, working parties were found and work was carried on under R,E, supervision at S,7,d,8,15, and S,9,d,8,15, (Sheet 36c,S,W,)	
			Major H,M,C,Curtis took over the command of the Battalion on the 19th October 1917 when Lt, Col, J,Stuart Wortley proceeded on leave to England,	

In the field,
31st October 1917,

Medlock
MAJOR,
Commanding 2/6th Bn, South Staffordshire Regiment,

Army Form C. 2118.

WAR DIARY
or
INTELLIGENCE SUMMARY.
(Erase heading not required.)

WD 10

P. 10

Original War Diary
of
76th Punjabis Staff Regiment

from 1st Nov 1917.
to 30th Nov 1917.

Secret Confidential

Army Form C. 2118.

Instructions regarding War Diaries and Intelligence
Summaries are contained in F.S. Regs., Part II.
and the Staff Manual respectively. Title pages
will be prepared in manuscript.

WAR DIARY
or
INTELLIGENCE SUMMARY.
(Erase heading not required.)

Sheet 1

Place	Date	Hour	Summary of Events and Information	Remarks and references to Appendices
SOUCHEZ	Nov 1st		(Sheet 36 c SW-3.8 c W3-1) Billeted in huts:	
			The Corps Commander awarded Military Medals to the undermentioned N.C.O. and men in connection with recent operations in the YPRES Sector:	
			2/6th South Staffordshire Regt:	
			240020 Sgt Jones E. A Coy	
			1845 Pte Simcox E. A Coy	
			241907 Pte Knight W. B Coy	
			Divisional Cards have been awarded to the following N.C.O's and men for conspicuous in the field:	
			242129 L/Cpl Everton H. C Coy	
			2.681 Pte Bishop W. H. C Coy	
			242271 Pte Cox W J D Coy	
			242157 Pte Cubb J' C Coy	
			242322 Pte Gatewel W G D Coy	
			241244 Pte Fernyhough J C Coy	
			241440 Pte Hickman P B Coy	
			242131 Pte Sperry A C Coy	
			The above were presented to ----- by the Divisional Commander.	
	Nov 2nd		Working parties were found under R.E. supervision:	
	Nov 3rd		Working parties under R.E. in Souchez area:	
	Nov 4th		ditto:	
	Nov 5th		Other Ranks - to Refinery:	
	Nov 6th		Working parties under R.E. in Souchez area:	
			On the night of the 6/7th this Unit relieved the 2/5th N.S.F & Derby Regt on Lock up	
			Support position in RED TRENCH in the AVION SECTOR.	
	Nov 7th, 8th & 9th - Working parties in front line trenches and C.T:		
	Nov 10th A Coy moved back from position in RED TRENCH to a position in GIVENCHY, owing to change in disposition on the Brigade front:		
	Nov 10th, 11th & 12th - Working parties in front line trenches and C.T:		
	Nov 13th/14th - This battalion relieved the 2/5th South Staffords Regt in the front line: C Coy on the front right Coy and D Coy the front left Coy.		
	November 15th		A Coy relieved C Coy in front line	
			B Coy relieved D C Y in front line	
	Nov 17/18th relieved by the 13th Canadian Bat. and marched out to SOUCHEZ CAMP:		

Army Form C. 2118.

WAR DIARY
or
INTELLIGENCE SUMMARY.

Sheet 2

(Erase heading not required.)

Instructions regarding War Diaries and Intelligence Summaries are contained in F. S. Regs., Part II. and the Staff Manual respectively. Title pages will be prepared in manuscript.

Place	Date	Hour	Summary of Events and Information	Remarks and references to Appendices
SOUCHEZ	Nov 19th		The Battalion Marched from SOUCHEZ to SIMENCOURT arriving at 6pm – the battalion was accommodated in huts: (Map – LENS II)	
SIMENCOURT	Nov 20/21st		Battalion resting and cleaning up:	
	Nov 22nd		The Battalion marched at 12.30 am to COUTURELLES + N – COMPTE and was accommodated in huts:	
COUTURELLES LE – COMPTE	Nov 23rd		The Battalion marched to SOMBRIN arriving at 6pm and arrived at HERMIES to be on detraining the battalion marched to HAPLINCOURT (W 15 Map 57 C) were it was accommodated in huts:	
HAPLINCOURT	Nov 24th/27th		The battalion remained at Haplincourt and continued training:	
	Nov 27th		The battalion marched to the Ravine at a.9.c.6. (57c) were it was bivouaced for the night:	
	Nov 28th/29		The battalion relieved the 2nd Batt Coldstream Guards in support trenches in the S.W. of BOURLON WOOD F 13 C & D (57c): Capt R.M Sheppard C'mdg C Coy was wounded:	
BOURLON WOOD	Nov 29th		Enemy heavily bombarded Bourlon Wood with H.E and gas shells and attacked at dawn the positions of the 2/6th North Staff Regt front, to which we were in support: Coy of this battalion advanced through the wood under heavy fire and reinforced the front line in answer to the S O S signal: Capt H Yeatman C'mdg A Coy was wounded and gassed and Lt. ... the Coy	
	Nov 30th		Continued several gas casualties: The Battalion was heavily bombarded by gas and H E shells and Capt H S Atkinson C'mdg C whole of "C" & D" Coys becoming casualties was killed. During these two days the battalion suffered heavy casualties from gas, the Capt J H Hendon Capt C E L Whitehouse and Lt P F S Eggle were gassed: A F Brown was wounded:	

In the field.
7th November 1917

Signed [signature]
Lieut-Col:
C'mdg 2/6th South Staff Graff's Regt:

Army Form C. 2118.

WAR DIARY
or
INTELLIGENCE SUMMARY.

(Erase heading not required.)

Original

War Diary
of
16th South Staffs Regiment

From 1st Dec 1917
to 31st Dec 1917

Confidential

Army Form C. 2118.

WAR DIARY
or
INTELLIGENCE SUMMARY

(Erase heading not required.)

Instructions regarding War Diaries and Intelligence Summaries are contained in F. S. Regs, Part II and the Staff Manual respectively. Title Pages will be prepared in manuscript.

Place	Date	Hour	Summary of Events and Information	Remarks and references to Appendices
BOURLON WOOD:	Dec. 1st:		The Battalion which was in support to 2/6th:North Staffs:Regt: at Bourlon Wood was relieved by 2/4th:Leicester Regt:.	
FLESQUERES:	Dec.2nd:		Battalion arrived at FLESQUERES at 4:a:m: about 150 strong: Accommodated in the Chateau:	
RIBECOURT:	Dec.3rd:		The Battalion moved back to RIBECOURT Ravine where Transport & Details were situated: Accommodated in bivouacs:	
HAVRINCOURT:	Dec.4th:		Move to HAVRINCOURT by march route, cross country, leaving Ribecourt at 12 midnight:	
	Dec.5th:		Battalion accommodated in a dug-out: from 5:a:m: till 12 noon: Bombing raid by enemy air-craft: one man injured: Moved by march route, across country to YTRES arriving at 4:p:m: Billetted in huts in LITTLE WOOD CAMP:	
YTRES:	Dec. 6th:		Resting:	
"	Dec. 7th:		Bathing: cleaning up etc: Medical Inspection by A:D:M:S: 59th:Division: of all men who had been in Bourlon Wood:	
"	Dec. 8th:		Bathing continued: Inspection parades:	
"	Dec. 9th:		Church Parades:	
"	Dec. 10th:		Orders received that Battalion, less transport, was to proceed to RUE near ABBEVILLE: Entrained at YTRES at 4:p:m: 2/Lieut;Newcombe was left in charge of Transport:	
RUE:	Dec. 11th:		Arrived at RUE at 4:a:m: Men billeted in schools, barns etc: Lt:Col:J:Stuart Wortley appointed C:O: Troops, (2/5th:South Staffs: 2/6th:North Staffs, 176th:L:T:M:Battery):	
"	Dec. 12th to Dec. 14th:		Bathing Parties to ABBEVILLE:	
"	Dec. 15th:		Draft of 30 O:R: arrived: Bathing at Acceville: Major;Curtis proceeded on leave to PARIS: Reading and recreation room opened:	

2449 Wt. W14957/M90 750,000 1/16 J.B.C. & A. Forms/C.2118/12.

Army Form C. 2118.

WAR DIARY
or
INTELLIGENCE SUMMARY

(Erase heading not required.)

Instructions regarding War Diaries and Intelligence
Summaries are contained in F. S. Regs., Part II.
and the Staff Manual respectively. Title Pages
will be prepared in manuscript.

Place	Date	Hour	Summary of Events and Information	Remarks and references to Appendices
RUE:	Dec:16th:		Church Parade for Nonconformists:	
"	Dec:17th:		Bathing at Abbeville: 241205:Pte:Evans:J: D:Coy: awarded the Military Medal for bravery at Bourlon Wood:	
"	Dec:18th: to Dec:22nd:		Bathing at Abbeville daily: Lt:Col:J:Stuart Wortley proceeded to PARIS on leave: Major H:M:C:Curtis in Command:	
"	Dec:23rd:		Church parades:	
"	Dec:24th:		No Parades: Bathing at Abbeville:	
"	Dec:25th:		Church Parades: Christmas dinner served by Companies: Extras and Geese bought by Regimental Funds and grant of 600 Francs: from Divisional Canteen:	
"	Dec:26th:		No parades: Bathing at Abbeville:	
"	Dec:27th:		Bathing at Abbeville: Medical Inspection:	
"	Dec:28th:		Staffs:Regiment: Parades for fit men: Four Officers joined from the 4th:battn:South	
"	Dec:30th:		Church Parades:	
"	Dec:31st:		Reinforcements arrived: 5 Officers and 450 O.R: arrived 3.a.m: from Depot Battalion: A: C: & D:Coys: reorganised, the following Officers in command:-	
			A:Coy: Capt:T:L:Astoury:	
			C:Coy: Capt:W:S:Lynes:	
			D:Coy: Capt:A:Adam:	

Final check or casualties:-Officers: 1 killed: 3 wounded: 14 Gassed:
O.R: 13 killed: Wounded & Gassed: 392: Missing: 15:
(Of the 392 wounded and gassed 64 have died):

In the field:
4th:January:1918:

Mur Wortley, LIEUT:COLONEL:
Commanding: 2/6th:Battn:South Staffordshire Regt:

2449 Wt. W14957/Mgo 750,000 1/16 J.B.C. & A. Forms/C.2118/12.

Army Form C. 2118.

WAR DIARY
or
INTELLIGENCE SUMMARY.
(Erase heading not required.)

Original

War Diary

of

16th Bn South Staffs Regiment

From 1st Jan 1916
To 31st Jan 1916

Confidential

P.12

CONFIDENTIAL!

Instructions regarding War Diaries and Intelligence Summaries are contained in F.S. Regs., Part II. and the Staff Manual respectively. Title pages will be prepared in manuscript.

Army Form C. 2118.

WAR DIARY
or
INTELLIGENCE SUMMARY.
(Erase heading not required.)

Place	Date	Hour	Summary of Events and Information	Remarks and references to Appendices
RUE:	1/1/18:		Morning Route March and afternoon kit inspection: Bathing: The following congratulatory message received from V Corps Commander:-	
			"On the withdrawal of the 59th:Division from the line, and on its departure from the V Corps the Corps Commander wishes me to say that he much appreciates the good work done by the Division during the time it has been under his command. The Division has used experience gained, to its advantage, and has throughout a difficult period, shewn good fighting qualities. Orders issued, both with regard to battle and work, havebeen carried out with cheerfulness and entirely in the right spirit: The Corps Commander will be glad to have the Division again in the Corps: He wishes all ranks a happy Christmas"	
			(sd) G:F:Boyd: B:G: G:S: V Corps: 22/12/17:	
			With reference to the above the G.O.C: 176th:Bde: sent the following message:-	
			" The Brigade Commander is glad to be able to forward the accompanying memorandum from the G:O:C: V Corps: He wishes the memorandum to be read by Company Commanders to their men, so that all ranks may know the good work they have done is appreciated:"	
do:	3 - 5/1/18:		Usual parades for Specialists: Bathing daily: Lieut:E:E:Owens:R:A:M:C: previously Medical Officer awarded Military Cross: Capt;W:A:Adam joined; in command of "D" Company: On 4th: all men who were in Bourlon Wood were inspected by D:A:D:M:S: G:O:C: 59th:Division inspected billets:	
do:	6th:		Church Parades:	
do:	7,8,9,10th:		Usual morning parades: Bathing daily: Inclement weather interrupted parades on several occasions:	

Army Form C. 2118.

WAR DIARY
or
INTELLIGENCE SUMMARY.
(Erase heading not required.)

Instructions regarding War Diaries and Intelligence Summaries are contained in F. S. Regs., Part II. and the Staff Manual respectively. Title pages will be prepared in manuscript.

Place	Date	Hour	Summary of Events and Information	Remarks and references to Appendices
RUE:	11/1/18:		Morning Parades: Men who were in Bourlon Wood inspected by A:D:M:S: 59th: Division:	
do:	12th:		Morning Parades:. G:O:C: 176th:Infantry Brigade inspected billets:	
do:	13th:		Church Parades: Inspection during the afternoon by D:M:S: 3rd:Army: & D:D:M:S: VIth: Corps for remainder of men who were in Bourlon Wood: 50 present:	
do:	14th:		50 Signallers under 2/Lieut:Newcombe left Rue to rejoin the Brigade: Captain joined from 1/6th:Bn:South Staffs:Regiment and took over Command of "C" Company: Usual morning parades and bathing at Abbeville:	
do:	15th:		Morning parades and bathing: Captain & Adjutant:C:E:L:Whitehouse: rejoined unit from Base:	
do:	16th:		Usual parades: 16 Officers joined ex: Depot Battalion and THird line:	
do:	17th:		do.:	
do:	18th:		do.: Concerts in afternoon and evening in Twon Hall Miss Lena Ashwell's Party:	
do:	19th:		Battalion route march in conjunction with 2/6th:Bn:North Staffs:Regiment to LE CROTOY: Returned to Rue at 8:p:m:	
do:	20th:		Church Parades:	
do:.	21st:		Morning parades: Advance party of 5 Officers and 5 N:C:Os: left Rue to proceed to BEAUFORT:	
do:	22nd:		Battalion left Rue at 11:a:m: for BEAUFORT: via: Abbeville and Prevent: Arrived Prevent 6:p:m and proceeded by Light Railway to BEAUFORT arriving there at 8:p:m: Billeted in huts, barns etc:	
Beaufort:	23rd:		No parades; Cleaning billets etc:	

Army Form C. 2118.

WAR DIARY
or
INTELLIGENCE SUMMARY.
(*Erase heading not required.*)

Instructions regarding War Diaries and Intelligence Summaries are contained in F. S. Regs., Part II. and the Staff Manual respectively. Title pages will be prepared in manuscript.

Place	Date	Hour	Summary of Events and Information	Remarks and references to Appendices
Beaufort.	24/1/18:		Training commenced: Specialist classes started:	
do:	25th:		Training continued: Morning parades: Afternoon Recreational Training: Tactical scheme for Signallers under Brigade arrangements:	
do:	26th:		Training continued: Recreational training in afternoon:	
do:	27th:		Church parades: Church of England at MANIN:	
do:	28th:		Training: 2 companies only: Bathing for remainder:at BERLENCOURT:	
do:	29th:		ditto:	
do:	30th:		Inspection of the Battalion by G.O.C: 176th:Infantry Brigade: Parades by companies: Transport inspected also:	
			During the afternoon a Cross Country Run took place, arranged by 176th:Inf: Bde: Whole Battalion took part each company starting at quarter of hour intervals: "C" Company won, with 47% of starters in at a given time:	
do:	31st:		Usual parades carried out: Firing on range: Commanding Officer, Adjutant & Company Commanders proceeded to visit prospective Battalion front in the Bullecourt sector:	
HONOURS & AWARDS:			London Gazette 28/12/17: Awarded the Distinguished Service Order: MAJOR:H:M:C:CURTIS: 241208:SGT:GOODEY:A:T: Awarded the Distinguished Conduct Medal:	
Mentioned in Sir:Douglas Haig's Despatch 7/11/17: Major:H:M:C:Curtis: Capt:R:M:Sheppard: C.S:M:Aston: & Private Perks:				
B:E:F: France:			LT: COLONEL:	
1/1/1918:			Commanding:2/6th:Bn:South Staffs: Regiment:	

[signature]

59/176

Army Form C. 2118.

WAR DIARY
INTELLIGENCE SUMMARY.
(Erase heading not required.)

Vol 13

Confidential

Original

War Diary

of

2/6th Bn. South Staffs Regiment

From :- 1st July 1918
To :- 28th July 1918

Army Form C. 2118.

CONFIDENTIAL.

Instructions regarding War Diaries and Intelligence Summaries are contained in F. S. Regs., Part II. and the Staff Manual respectively. Title Pages will be prepared in manuscript.

WAR DIARY
or
INTELLIGENCE SUMMARY

(Erase heading not required.)

Place	Date	Hour	Summary of Events and Information	Remarks and references to Appendices
Beaufort.	1..2..18.		Training continued. Specialist Classes. Tactical Scheme for Signals, Scouts and Staffs. Afternoon - Recreational Training.	
	2..2..18.		Morning Parades only.	
	3..2..18.		Church Parades.	
	4..2..18.		Brigade Route March. 8.a.m. - 12.30.p.m. Afternoon - Fitting Small Box Respirators.	
	5..2..18.		Inspection of Brigade by G.O.C. VIth.Corps. Battalion Band played the General Salute.	
	6..2..18.		Morning Parades and Bathing. Sergeant.King.H.R. "A" Coy. and Cpl.Bowler.H. "C" Coy. awarded Belgian Croix de Guerre for gallantry at Ypres.	
	7..2..18.		Morning Parades and Bathing.	
Pommier.	8..2..18.		Battalion moved by march route to POMMIER. Left Beaufort 8.a.m. arriving Pommier 12 noon. Billetted in barns etc.	
	9..2..18.		Move by march route to MORY via. Courcelles-le-Compte. Left Pommier 7.30.a.m. arrived MORY 4.p.m. Battalion in huts in Mory South Camp. Transport and Q.M.Stores at Dysart Camp.	
Mory.	10..2..18.		Battalion left Mory Camp 4.30.p.m. and proceeded to the line and took over Right Sector of Brigade Front, Noreuil, from 14th.Highland Light Infantry and 14th. Argylls & Sutherland Highlanders. Two Companies in the front line; 1 Company in reserve and one company in support.	
	11..2..18.		Quiet day. One casualty.	
	12..2..18.		Situation very quiet.	
	13..2..18.		Situation very quiet. Shelling during evening. 4 Officers & 90. O.R. (draft from 8th.Bn. South Staffs.Regt) joined Battalion in the line.	
	14..2..18.		Situation very quiet till about 7.p.m. when heavy enemy shelling commenced. Gas shells mixed with High Explosive. Gas projection on our front line. Gas casualties, 1 Officer and 50 O.R. (2/Lieut.E.B.Proud gassed). 12 of gas casualties died.	
	15..2..18.		Quiet all day.	
	16..2..18.		Situation normal. Considerable aerial activity. Four enemy machines brought down on our front. Battalion relieved by 5th.Bn.North Staffordshire Regiment. Battalion returned to Mory South Camp.	

2449 Wt. W14957/M90 750,000 1/16 J.B.C. & A. Forms/C.2118/12.

WAR DIARY
or
INTELLIGENCE SUMMARY
(Erase heading not required.)

Army Form C. 2118.

Place	Date	Hour	Summary of Events and Information	Remarks and references to Appendices
MORY.	17..2..18.		Battalion Resting. Cleaning up in afternoon. Working party of 50. O.R. for work at Brigade Transport Lines. Working Party of 4 Officers and 300 O.R. left Mory Camp 4.p.m. for work on Dewsbury Trench. Lt.Col.J.Stuart Wortley proceeded on leave to England. Major.H.M.C.Curtis in Command. Captain.W.A.Adam acting as Second in Command.	
	18..2..18.		Working Parties resting. Special Bayonet Fighting Class for 4 Off. and 12 O.R. held daily for 4½ days under Birgade Physical Drill Instructor. Specialist Training. Enemy aircraft very active at night. Bombing raid from 8.15.p.m. - 10.p.m. and several dropped in vicinity of Camp. No casualties.	
	19..2..18.		Church Parade in MORY Theatre. Companies bathing. Specialist Training carried on. 2/Lieut.Twomey proceeded to England for transfer to Machine Gun Corps.	
	20..2..18.		Specialist Training. Companies instructed in Rapid Wiring. Three companies on Working Party at night on Dewsbury Trench.	
	21..2..18.		Specialist Training. "A" Coy. - Rapid Wiring. Lieuts.K.Davies & W.Horton proceeded to England for 6 months tour of duty at home.	
	22..2..18.		Commanding Officer's Inspection of Companies in Fighting Order. Preparations for proceeding to line. Battalion left Mory Camp 5.p.m. and relieved 2/6th.Bn.North Staffordshire Regiment in Left Sub-Sector of Brigade Front. (Noreuil). Two companies in Front-Line. 1 Company in Support and one in Reserve.	
	23..2..18.		Situation quiet. Few Gas Shells fell near "B" Coy. Headquarters. Casualties - Nil.	
	24..2..18.		Shelling near Battalion H.Qs. and heavy barrage put down on reserves during the day. Casualties - 2.O.R. wounded by shell and 1 O.R. slight.	
	25..2..18.		Quiet. Intended raid by 5th.North Staffs.Regt. cancelled owing to moonlight. Our own Artillery hit one of our posts at 9.p.m. Casualties - nil.	
	26..2..18.		Situation quiet. Enemy aircraft active over our lines. Reserve Coy. transferred from Igaree Corner to Railway Reserve (near Battn.H.Q.) to make room for portion of Reserve Battalion. Casualties - nil.	
	27..2..18.		Headquarters shelled during afternoon. 2/6th.North Staffs.Regt. (1 Off. 11.O.R) raided enemy post for purpose of obtaining identification. Raiding party left our line 3.a.m. but found enemy post unoccupied. Casualties - nil.	
	28..2..18.		Enemy aeroplane over our line 11.a.m. - driven off by Machine Gun fire. Support Trench shelled during afternoon.	

[signature] MAJOR.

59th Division.
176th Infantry Brigade.

WAR DIARY

2/6th BATTALION

THE SOUTH STAFFORDSHIRE REGIMENT

MARCH 1 9 1 8

Army Form C. 2118.

59/7

WAR DIARY
or
INTELLIGENCE SUMMARY.

(Erase heading not required.)

WD 14

Confidential

Original

War Diary
of
2/6th Bn. South Staffs Regiment

from 1st March 1918
to 31st March 1918

P. 14

Army Form C. 2118.

WAR DIARY
or
INTELLIGENCE SUMMARY.
(Erase heading not required.)

Instructions regarding War Diaries and Intelligence Summaries are contained in F.S. Regs, Part II. and the Staff Manual respectively. Title pages will be prepared in manuscript.

Place	Date	Hour	Summary of Events and Information	Remarks and references to Appendices
	1st.March to night 6/7th.		The Battalion occupied the Front Line of the Left Sub-Sector of Brigade Front, NOREUIL. Casualties slight. Relieved in the front line by the 5th.Bn.North Staffs.Regiment, and accommodated in Support Line at IGAREE CORNER, PONMISTRACT & DEWKSBURY TRENCHES.	
	7th. to night of 10/11th.		The Battalion occupied the Support line till the night of 10/11th, when they were relieved by the 7th.Bn.Notts and Derby Regt. On relief they returned to MORY,Le Abbaye Camp and were accommodated in Huts. Lt.Col.J.Stuart Wortley returned from leave on the 9th.inst.	
	10th.		Draft of 82 O.R. reported from 8th.Bn.South Staffs.Regt.	
	10th. to night of 19/20th.		Battalion was in Brigade Reserve; men employed in cleaning up etc, bathing: Specialist classes were commenced. Large Working Parties were found nightly for digging and wiring in Defence Systems. On several mornings the enemy shelled the vicinity of the Camp with H.E. Battalion had "Stand To" each morning, and on the morning of 13th. and 18th. they moved to reserve Line of Defence near ECOUST but returned to Camp on each occasion about 8.a.m.	
	19th.		Battalion left MORY Le Abbaye Camp at 5.p.m. and relieved 2/4th.Leicester Regt. in Left Brigade Sector, Right Sub-Sector, BULLECOURT.	
	20th.		Situation normal. No casualties.	
	21st.		Heavy enemy shelling of back areas commenced between 2 & 3.a.m. also heavy bombardment by enemy of Front & Support Line with H.E. and Gas Shells from 4.a.m. - 8.a.m. Enemy attacked in massed formation at 9.a.m. and succeeded in capturing the Front Line and also effected a flank move and got through to Railway Reserve and Battalion Headquarters. 23 Officers & about 500 O.R. are "Missing", including Lt.Col.J.Stuart Wortley, Capt.C.E.L. Whitehouse (Adjutant), Capt. W.A.Adam, Capt. W.A.Jordan, Capt. T.L.Astbury & Capt. W.S.Lynes, (Company Commanders). The following Officers are missing:- Lieut.W.T.Butler, Lieut.R.G.Boycott, Lieut. L.J.Shelton, 2/Lieut.H.P.Bunn, 2/Lt.H.E.Shipton, 2/Lt.H.W.Gregory, 2/Lt.J.A.Geyton, 2/Lt.R.Baxter, 2/Lt.F.W.Sniter, 2/Lt.C.Haworth, 2/Lt.T.A.Gough, 2/Lt.G.A.Yates, 2/Lt. J.Bonshor, 2/Lt.F.J.Rigby, 2/Lt.K.R.Jones, & Capt.W.M.Christie, R.A.M.C. The Q.M.Stores and Transport moved from Dysart Camp at 5.p.m. by march route via Coucelles-les- Compte to DOIGNY where they bivouaced.	

Army Form C. 2118.

WAR DIARY
or
INTELLIGENCE SUMMARY.
(*Erase heading not required.*)

Instructions regarding War Diaries and Intelligence Summaries are contained in F.S. Regs., Part II. and the Staff Manual respectively. Title pages will be prepared in manuscript.

Place	Date	Hour	Summary of Events and Information	Remarks and references to Appendices
	21st.		Major.H.M.C.Curtis. proceeded to the line with details from the Transport Lines, a party of 2 Officers (2/Lt.S.G.Maitland & 2/Lt.S.G.Bradbury) & 50 O.R. including Band and specialists under training and held a portion of the front line of the Third System of Defence, East of MORY. until relieved at 4.a.m. 22nd.	
	22nd.	4.a.m.	Major Curtis & party took up a position on the Army Line 500 yards N.E. of MORY and held this position all day in spite of heavy enemy shelling and attacks. Transport & Q.M.Stores still remained at DOUCHY.	
	23rd.	1.a.m.	Owing to the flanks being exposed and heavy enemy attacks the party under Major Curtis fell back 300 yards in a W.S.W. direction but owing to repeated attacks, and being isolated had again to withdraw. The party dug in on ridge covering ERVILLERS and held this position till relieved by the Suffolks. The remainder of the party then marched to MIRAUMONT and entrained to KIEBEM at 9.p.m. Transport, Stores etc. marched from DOUCHY at 9.a.m. and arrived at BOUZINCOURT at 6.p.m. Major Curtis & party rejoined Transport and Stores at BOUZINCOURT where the Battalion remained.	
	24th.			
	25th.	2.a.m.	Battalion left BOUZINCOURT at 2.a.m. and proceeded by march route to BEAUCOURT arriving there at 5.a.m. Men billetted in Barns etc.	
	26th.		Left BEAUCOURT at 7.a.m. and proceeded by march route to CANDAS arriving at 1.p.m. Billetted in barns etc.	
	27th.		Unit still at CANDAS. Bathing.	
	28th. 29th.		Battalion (less Transport) entrained at 12 noon. Transport left at 8.a.m. and proceeded by road. Battalion detrained at AUVIGNEY and proceeded by lorries to GAUCHIN-LEGAL arriving at 6.a.m. and billetted in the Chateau. Transport arrived at 5.p.m.	
	30th.		H.M.The King inspected the Battalion and billets at Chateau at 9.30.a.m. Draft of 40 O.R. joined unit from 8th.Bn.South Staffs.Regt.	
	31st.		Transport left by road for WATAU. Church parades held.	

Army Form C. 2118.

WAR DIARY
or
INTELLIGENCE SUMMARY.
(Erase heading not required.)

Instructions regarding War Diaries and Intelligence Summaries are contained in F. S. Regs., Part II. and the Staff Manual respectively. Title pages will be prepared in manuscript.

Place	Date	Hour	Summary of Events and Information	Remarks and references to Appendices
	31st.		The following extract from a letter addressed to the Divisional Commander by Lieut-General Sir.J.Aylmer Haldane, K.C.B. D.S.O. Commanding VIth.Corps was received:-	
			"Will you please convey to all ranks of your Division my admiration and thanks for the very gallant stand they made against overwhelming numbers of the enemy supported by a tremendous artillery.	
			The Division nobly did their duty on the right of the VIth.Corps, and from all accounts that have reached me have inflicted heavy loss upon the enemy. I grieve for the heavy casualties among your gallant officers, N.C.Os. and men but the 59th.Division have the satisfaction of knowing that they did their duty in as trying circumstances as can possibly happen in war.	
			In the field.	
			6.4.18.	
			MAJOR.	
			Commanding.2/5th.Battalion South Staffordshire Regiment.	

176th Brigade.

59th Division.

==========

2/6th BATTALION

SOUTH STAFFORDSHIRE REGIMENT

APRIL 1918.

Army Form C. 2118.

WAR DIARY
or
INTELLIGENCE SUMMARY.
(Erase heading not required.)

Original

War Diary
of
2/6th Bn. South Staffs Regiment

From 1st April 1918
to 30th April 1918

Introduction

Army Form C. 2118.

Most Confidential

WAR DIARY
or
INTELLIGENCE SUMMARY.

(Erase heading not required.)

Instructions regarding War Diaries and Intelligence Summaries are contained in F.S. Regs., Part II. and the Staff Manual respectively. Title pages will be prepared in manuscript.

Place	Date	Hour	Summary of Events and Information	Remarks and references to Appendices
Gauchin Légal	1.4.18	—	The Battalion left Gauchin Légal 7am. marched to Hersin, arrived Proven 7 pm. marched to Watou arriving at 9 p.m.; strength of 150 O.R. arrived 11 pm.	
Watou	2.4.18		Company parades; cleaning up etc; specialist training. Transport arrived 2 p.m. strength of 173 O.R.	
"	3.4.18		Training continued. Inspection by G.O.C. 2nd army in afternoon. strength of 127 O.R.	
"	4.4.18		Training continued. strength 97 O.R.	
"	5.4.18		Training continued. Lewis Gunners no company firing on range. Inspection of boys by G.O.C. The following message received from G.O.C. 2nd Third Army:- "I cannot allow the 59th Division to leave the Third army without expressing my appreciation of their splendid conduct during the great battle which is first concluded. By their devotion and courage they have worn up overwhelming attacks and prevented the enemy gaining his object, namely, a decisive victory. I wish them every possible good luck. (Sd) J. Byng, General." Training continued. Lewis Gunners and company on range. strength 157 O.R.	
"	6.4.18		Training Gas Schimitz; Church parade.	
"	7.4.18		Training firing on range. G.O.C. Brigade inspected drafts	
"	8.4.18		—do—	
"	9.4.18		Battalion left camp 9.30am marched to Poperinghe; thence by train to Quintin Sars; marched to Ubrican Camp, Ypres; arrived 2.30pm. Transport moved by road + arrived at Brandehoek 5pm; enemy shelling.	
Ypres	10.4.18		Battalion left Camp 6.45pm relieved 18th K.R.R. in dugouts in Left Bele Sector, Passchendaele	
"	11.4.18		Sector at 11 p.m.; slight enemy shelling.	

Army Form C. 2118.

WAR DIARY
or
INTELLIGENCE SUMMARY.
(Erase heading not required.)

(2)

Instructions regarding War Diaries and Intelligence Summaries are contained in F. S. Regs., Part II. and the Staff Manual respectively. Title pages will be prepared in manuscript.

Place	Date	Hour	Summary of Events and Information	Remarks and references to Appendices
Passchendaele	12.4.18		Quiet all day; enemy aircraft active in afternoon running Baro received from Battalion to withdraw from line at surplus stores not able to be removed were distroyed. Baron returned to Keilzig Lin entrenched at 11 pm. Retunnels Bunghalor. Was marched to Brake hunts, Vlamertinghe where transport R.Q.M. store's dinner awaits.	
	13.4.18		Moved by march route at 11 am to Reninghelst; Battalion in Ontario Camp are to form.	
Vlamertinghe				
Reninghelst	14.4.18		Left camp 3 am marched to LOCRE arriving at 8 am, billeted in huts, in reserve.	
Locre	15.4.18		Battalion proceeded to line 12 midnight & took up new position from 9th Bde SE of Bailleul at 1.30 pm. Enemy shelled Bailleul heavily from 11 am onwards etc 2 pm. Enemy attacked on our left line also repulsed. At 3.30 pm enemy put down a heavy barrage in rear of our line & attacked & succeeded in getting thro' on left flank causing Battn to retire West of Bailleul where we fell back on to a hastily prepared line 1½ Kilos W of Bailleul; this position was held in spite of heavy enemy shelling M.G. & rifle fire until relief line held by Royal Scots in rear, was able to offer a determined resistance. The Battalion proceeded to Canada Corner Camp arriving about midnight however during the situation area; 1 Officer killed (2/Lt. G. Thwaites), 2 Officers wounded (2/Lts. Blumer & J. Renard), & 90 O.R. killed wounded & missing. During day Transport R.Q.M. stores has been heavily shelled; was ordered up & 2 Cavalry records left LOCRE 11pm proceeded Ontario Camp Reninghelst arriving 2.30 a.m. 16th.	
Locre	16.4.18 17.4.18		Battalion in reserve; camp was shelled several times had to be vacated. Transport lines at Ringinghalo also heavily shelled.	
	18.4.18		Shelling heavy; Battalion left at 12 noon marched to TERDEGHEM, arr. drummerode billeted in huts previously VIIIth Korps detond, arrived 6 pm.	

WAR DIARY or INTELLIGENCE SUMMARY

Army Form C. 2118.

Place	Date	Hour	Summary of Events and Information	Remarks and references to Appendices
Terdeghem	19.4.18		Battalion left TER DEGHEM 11 am marched to S.W. of Proven; billeted in huts at Minor Camp, Blaringhe at 6 pm.	
Blaringhe	20.4.18		Cleaning up etc. Enemy aircraft bombing at night.	
"	21.4.18		Left camp 7 am marched to ROUSBRUGGE arriving at 11 am; billeted in huts; cleaning up during aircraft bombed camp; 1 off. wounded (2/Lt L. Oldroyd); 5 O.R. killed, 7 wounded.	
Rousbrugge	22.4.18		Coy. parades in morning; moved to Beaver Chappe camp at 4 pm.	
"	23.4.18		Coy. parades. Marking. Lecture to all officers re N.C.Os by G.O.C. Division. Draft of 17 officers + 60 O.R. joined unit.	
	24.4.18 25.4.18		Training; doing two schemes. 2+2075 Sgt. Bot. B.G. - B.Coy awarded Military Medal.	
	26.4.18		Training; tactical schemes for officers. N.C.Ops. signalling. orderlies. wounded. 1 mile S.W. of Poperinghe. Seven left camp 5.45 pm marched to W. of Reminghelst having arrived line of French to line along railway in day. In reserve.	
Poperinghe	27.4.18		Bn. moved to W. of Reminghelst 7.30 pm.	
Reminghelst	28.4.18		Battalion received Reminghelst - Unknown reserve line - Heavy enemy barrage on front line - S.O.S. sent up. Battalion "stood to" at 7.30 pm. Situation quiet at 9 pm. 5 O.R. killed.	
	29.4.18		Battalion still in reserve; heavy artillery activity on both sides - 6 R. wounded, 5 shaved.	
	30.4.18		Battalion in reserve; heavy enemy shelling at 4:30 pm. 2 O.R. wounded, 1 shaved.	

M.Clark
Lt. Colonel
Commanding 2/North Bn. South Staffs. Regiment.

SECRET & CONFIDENTIAL.

WAR DIARY.

2/6TH. BATTALION SOUTH STAFFORDSHIRE REGIMENT. (TRAINING CADRE).

From:- May. 1st. 1918.
To:- May. 31st. 1918.

Army Form C. 2118.

WAR DIARY
or
INTELLIGENCE SUMMARY.

(Erase heading not required.)

Instructions regarding War Diaries and Intelligence Summaries are contained in F. S. Regs., Part II. and the Staff Manual respectively. Title pages will be prepared in manuscript.

Place	Date	Hour	Summary of Events and Information	Remarks and references to Appendices
Reninghelst.	1st.		Reserve. The Battalion still in support in the Reninghelst - Ouderdom Reserve Line. Slight enemy shelling - Working party of 3 Off. & 300 O.R. under R.E.supervision. Lt.Col.H.M.C.Curtis. D.S.O. awarded Bar to D.S.O. 2/Lieut.S.G.Maitland awarded Military Cross. Casualties during day:- 3 killed, 6 wounded.	
do.	2nd.		3 Off. 300. O.R. working party under R.E.supervision. - 1 O.R. killed.	
do.	3rd.		3 Off. 400. O.R. working party under R.E.supervision. - 7 O.R. killed.	
do.	4th.		4 Off. 200. O.R. do. on Defence Line. - Own artillery very active.	
do.	5th.		Battalion moved from Reninghelst and proceeded by March Route to Camp near Watou; billetted at Trappiste Farm; arrived 7.p.m. in heavy rain. - Transport & Q.M. stores moved from near Poperinghe to same camp. - 2 casualties, wounded, before Bn. left the line.	
Watou.	6th.		Transport left Camp. 10.a.m. and proceeded by road. - bivouaced at Rousbruck for the night. Battalion left Camp 3.p.m. and embussed at Watou. Arrived at Camp at Lederzeele at 8.p.m. 3 miles from St.Momelin.	
Lederzeele.	7th.		Cleaning up; Coy. parades. Instructions received for personnel of Battalion to be sent to Base.	
do.	8th.		Coy. parades etc. Preparations for departure of personnel for Base.	
do.	9th.		Battalion parade. Address by G.O.C. 59th.Division, who distributed the following decorations:- Bar to D.S.O. - Lt.Col.H.M.C.Curtis. D.S.O. Military Cross - 2/Lieut.S.G.Maitland. Belgian Croix de Guerre - 242176.Sgt.King.H.R. do. 16832.Sgt.Bowler.T. Military Medal. - 242075.Cpl.Coe.H.G. (att.176th.Inf.Bde). do. 242310.Pte.Wren.A. (att.176th.L.T.M.B). do. 201823.Cpl.Burgess.H. (att.176th.L.T.M.B). do. 242313.L/C.Chapman.A. (att.176th.Inf.Bde). Divisional Cards. 9597.Pte.Philpot.W.H. do.	

Army Form C. 2118.

WAR DIARY
or
INTELLIGENCE SUMMARY.

(Erase heading not required.)

Instructions regarding War Diaries and Intelligence Summaries are contained in F. S. Regs., Part II. and the Staff Manual respectively. Title pages will be prepared in manuscript.

Place	Date	Hour	Summary of Events and Information	Remarks and references to Appendices
Lederzeele.	9th.		18 Officers and 746. O.R. left Camp at 2.30.p.m; and proceeded by march route to Watten where they entrained for the Base. A Training Staff and Transport only remained; 11 Officers & 100 O.R. approx.	
do.	10th.		Training Cadre and Transport left Lederzeele at 6.a.m. and marched via. St.Omer to Mametz. Arrived 12 noon; billeted in barns etc.	
MAMETZ.	11th.		Left Mametz 7.30.a.m. and marched to FIEFS arriving at 12.30.p.m. - billetted in bar ns etc.	
FIEFS.	12th.		Church parade.	
do.	13th.		Orders for move received but cancelled; Bn. remained at Fiefs.	
do.	14th.		Training Cadre only left FIEFS at 9.30.a.m. and marched to MAGNICOURT-LE-COMTE - billetted at Houvelin. Transport left behind with Lieut.Carter and subsequently proceeded to 59th.Divn. Surplus Transport Concentration Camp, Etaples. (Battn. arrived Magnicourt 2.p.m.)	
MAGNICOURT-LE-COMTE.	15th.		Training Cadre left MAGNICOURT 9.30.a.m. and proceeded by march route to SOMBRIN; arrived 3.p.m. Camped in tents.	
SOMRIN.	16th.		Training Cadre took over Administration of the 2nd. & 3rd.Prov. Garrison Guard Battalions	
do.	17th. 18th. 19th.		Training; classes for Instructors of Training Cadre. Instructors sent to Battalions.	
do.	20th.		Bathing. Courses. Lieut.(A/Capt).R.J.I.Lane. (att.176th.L.T.M.B) awarded Bar to M.C. Lieut.J.H.Grice. (prev.att. 176th.L.T.B.) awarded Military Cross.	
do.	21st.		Left Camp at 5.a.m. and marched to MAGNICOURT-LE-COMTE, arriving at 11.30.a.m. Billetted in barns etc.	
MAGNICOURT-LE-COMTE.	22nd.		Left Magnicourt 7.a.m. and marched to Vielfort near HOUDAIN; Tents pitched in wood.	

Army Form C. 2118.

WAR DIARY
or
INTELLIGENCE SUMMARY.

(Erase heading not required.)

Instructions regarding War Diaries and Intelligence Summaries are contained in F. S. Regs., Part II. and the Staff Manual respectively. Title pages will be prepared in manuscript.

Place	Date	Hour	Summary of Events and Information	Remarks and references to Appendices
HOUDAIN.	23rd. 24th. 25th.		In Camp at Veilfort; Instruction in Gas.	
do.	26th.		Bathing.	
do.			Inspection. Training Cadre to be in readiness to move to 30th.Division at short notice. 240761.Pte.Chilton.R. A.Coy. reported Missing. 21..3..18. at Bullecourt arrived in United Kingdom 6..5..18. Prisoner of War escaped from territory occupied by enemy.	
do.	27th.		Training.	
do.	28th.		Training Cadre left Camp 3.30.p.m. and etrained at HOUDAIN.10.p.m.	
do.	29th.		Arrived NOYELLES at 7.p.m. Encamped in Rest Camp.	
NOYELLES.	30th.		Left Camp 10.a.m. and marched to BUIGNY -ST - MACLOU. Arrived 12.30.p.m. Battalion under orders of 198th.Infantry Brigade. 65th.Division. Capt.R.J.I.Lane. Joined Unit ex hospital and 176th.I.T.M.B.	
BUIGNY-ST-MACLOU.	31st.		Preparations made for arrival of American Regiment to whom Training Cadre is to be attached. Company "Training Cadres despatched to respective Training Areas:- A.Coy. (Capt.S.Bradbury). - PORT-LE-GRAND. B.Coy. (Capt.M.E.Williams). - NEUILLY-L'HOPITAL. C.Coy. (Lieut.J.H.Grice,M.C). - HAUTVILLIERS. D.Coy. (Capt.R.J.I.Lane,M.C). - ROMAINE. Headquarters and Stores remaining at BUIGNY-ST-MACLOU.	

LIEUT.COLONEL
Commanding.2/6th.Battalion South Staffs.Regiment.(Training Cadre)

SECRET & CONFIDENTIAL

2/6TH. BATTALION SOUTH STAFFORDSHIRE REGIMENT. (T.C.)

WAR DIARY.

From :- June. 1st. 1918.
To :- June. 30th. 1918.

Vol.

SECRET & CONFIDENTIAL.
Instructions regarding War Diaries and Intelligence
Summaries are contained in F.S. Regs., Part II.
and the Staff Manual respectively. Title pages
will be prepared in manuscript.

Army Form C. 2118.

WAR DIARY
or
INTELLIGENCE SUMMARY.

(Erase heading not required.)

JUNE 1918.

Place	Date	Hour	Summary of Events and Information	Remarks and references to Appendices
BUIGNY-ST-MACLOU.	1st. to 6th.		Battalion Training Cadre remained in Buigny-St-Maclou Area. American Units not arrived.	
do.	7th.		Battalion Training Cadre was relieved by 2/6th.B.Manchester Regt.Training Cadre, and proceeded by lorry to HELLICOURT. Left Buigny 1.p.m. arriving Hellicourt 5.30.p.m. Accommodated in tents in Camp with 1st.Bn. 325th.American Infantry Regt. B.Coy. Training Cadre was att. to Machine Gun Coy. 325th.Regt. at TILLOY FLORIVILLE. C.Coy. " " " " " " " " Headquarters, 325th.Infantry Regt. at HARCELLANES. Transport proceeded by road. Capt.R.J.I.Lane.M.C. proceeded on leave to England. Ca pt.E.W.Grant.(Chaplain) proceeded to join 5th.Bn.Welsh Regt, 176th.Infantry Brigade.	
HELLICOURT.	8th.		Transport arrived at 11.30.a.m.	
do.	10th. 11th.		Cadre assisted in training of American Units; practice in relief and manning of trenches. Gas N.C.Os. assisted in Gas Demonstration. The following were mentioned in Sir.Douglas Haig's Despatch of 7th.April.1918: LIEUT. COLONEL J.STUART WORTLEY. LIEUT.(A/CAPT). C.E.L.WHITEHOUSE. 242330.PTE.PERRY.A.S.	
do.	12th. 13th.14th.		Training Cadre assisting training of Americans; B.Coy. Cadre rejoined Unit. Training as usual.	
do.	15th.		1st.Bn.325.American Inf.Regt. left the Area. 4.p.m.	
do.	16th.		Church Service. C.Coy. Cadre rejoined Unit.	
do.	17th.		Training Cadre left Camp at 8.a.m. and marched to FRANLEU arriving 11.a.m. Relieved the 2/5th. Manchester Regt. Training Cadre, and attached to 3rd.Bn. 105th.American Infantry Regt. who arrived at Franleu at 5.p.m. Billeted in barns etc. B.Coy. Cadre detached at FRIBEULLES with one Company.	
FRANLEU.	18th.		Notification received that undermentioned Officers were posted to 2nd.Bn.South Staffs.Regt. Lieut.R.GRANT. att. 176th.Inf.Bde.H.Q., Lieut.R.E.GEE. att. 15th.Divn.Signals., Lieut.W.L. LAMAISON., att. 2/6th.North Staffs.Regt. T.C. Training of Americans commenced.	

Army Form C. 2118.

WAR DIARY
or
INTELLIGENCE SUMMARY.

(Erase heading not required.)

(2).

Instructions regarding War Diaries and Intelligence Summaries are contained in F. S. Regs., Part II. and the Staff Manual respectively. Title pages will be prepared in manuscript.

Place	Date	Hour	Summary of Events and Information	Remarks and references to Appendices
FRANLEU.	19th.		Battalion Training Cadre. left FRANLEU at 5.p.m. and marched to VISSE near Maisineres, arriving at 8.30.p.m. Billetted in barns etc. Attached to 90th.Infantry Brigade.	
VISSE.	20th.& 21st.		Training Cadre remained at VISSE.	
do.	22nd.		Training Cadre left VISSE at 9.a.m. and marched to BUSSUS-BUSSUE,approx. 40 kilos, arriving at 7.p.m. Billeted in barns etc. Attached to 2nd.Bn. 129th.American Infantry Regiment who arrived the same day.	
BUSSUS-BUSSUE.	23rd.		Morning devoted to cleaning up.	
do.	24th.&25th.		Training with Americans.	
do.	26th.		ditto. Capt.R.J.Lane.M.C. rejoined Unit from Xth.Corps.C.R.E.	
do.	27th.		rejoined Unit from Leave. Capt.J.A.Armstrong.M.C. Training continued. Americans firing on ranges at PONT REMY.	
do.	28th.) 29th.)		Training continued.	
do.	30th.		No parades.	

W. Churchill
LT.COLONEL.
Commanding. 2/6th.Battalion South Staffordshire Regiment. (T.C.)

CONFIDENTIAL.

WAR DIARY

OF

2/6th Battn. South Staffordshire Regt.

FROM.. 1st July 1918n TO:.. 31st July 1918.

VOLUME......

SECRET & CONFIDENTIAL.

Army Form C. 2118.

Instructions regarding War Diaries and Intelligence
Summaries are contained in F. S. Regs., Part II.
and the Staff Manual respectively. Title pages
will be prepared in manuscript.

WAR DIARY
or
INTELLIGENCE SUMMARY.

(Erase heading not required.)

Place	Date	Hour	Summary of Events and Information	Remarks and references to Appendices
BUSSUS - BUSSUEL.	July.1st.		Battalion Training Cadre still at Bussus-Bussuel assisting in the Training of the 2nd.Bn. 129th.American Infantry Regiment.	
	2nd.& 3rd.		Usual training; on 3rd. Battalion were firing on Rifle Range s at PONT REMY.	
	4th.		No parades; Holiday for the Americans in celebration of Independence Day. Sports and Concert held.	
	5th.		Usual parades in the morning; During the afternoon the 129th.American Infantry Regt. was inspected on the training ground by Mr.Lloyd.George, General Pershing & General Horne. Speech by Mr.Lloyd George.	
	6th.		No parades; American Bn. on route march.	
	7th.		No parades.	
	8th.		Usual training carried out. Small Box respirators tested. The following extract from London Gazette dated 3rd.June,1918. was published:- Lt.H.C.CARTER. - Awarded the Military Cross. 242302.L/Cpl.Eatwell.W.G.A. - Awarded the D.C.M.	
	9th.		Usual training.	
	10th.		Firing on range s at PONT REMY. - Gas Demonstration carried out at night.	
	11th.		Usual training; Night operations.	
	12th. & 13th.		Usual training carried out.	
	14th.		No parades.	
	15th.		Usual parades with Americans. The following extract from London Gazette dated 17th.June,1918. was published:- 241444.L/Cpl.SCREEN.T. 242052.Pte.MARTIN.T.A. Awarded the Meritorious Service Medal. ditto.	

Army Form C. 2118.

(2).

WAR DIARY
or
INTELLIGENCE SUMMARY.
(Erase heading not required.)

Instructions regarding War Diaries and Intelligence Summaries are contained in F.S. Regs., Part II. and the Staff Manual respectively. Title pages will be prepared in manuscript.

Place	Date	Hour	Summary of Events and Information	Remarks and references to Appendices
BUSSUS-BUSSUEL.	16th.		Usual training carried out.	
	17th.		The 2nd.Bn. 129th.American Infantry Regiment left Bussus-Bussuel Area at 8.a.m. Battalion Training Cadre remained.	
	18th.		Training for Cadre during the morning. Kit inspections in afternoon.	
	19th.		Training carried out during the morning.	
	20th.		Left Bussus-Bussuel at 9.30.a.m. and marched to COQUEREL, arriving at 11.30.a.m. Billetted in barns etc.	
COQUEREL.	21st.		Rifle Competition on Pont Remy Ranges	
	22nd.		Cadre left COQUEREL 4.p.m. and marched to PONT REMY; entrained 6.p.m. Arrived BLARGIES at 11.30.p.m. Under orders of 198th.Inf.Bde. Commanding Officer proceeded on leave.	
LANNOY-GUILLIERE.	23rd.		In Camp. and arrived at Camp at 2.a.m. In tents Camp about 2 kilos. from LANNOY-GUILLIERE.	
	24th.		Captain M.B.Williams, in command of the Cadre.	
	25th.		Preparations made for Training Cadre to proceed to Base but orders were subsequently cancelled. Training during morning. Capt. W.B.Allen, Adjutant, proceeded to India Office on duty. Lieut.	
	26 & 27th.		ditto. J.H.Grice acting as Adjutant.	
	28th.		Church Parades.	
	29 & 30th.		Morning parades and cleaning up.	
	31st.		Battalion training staff, less Officers, proceeded to Romescamps and entrained to join 2/6th. Battn. South Staffordshire Regiment. Left Camp. 8.a.m. From this date the 2/6th.Bn.South Staffordshire Regiment is disbanded.	

(signature) LT. COLONEL.

Commanding. 2/6th.Bn.South Staffordshire Regiment.